THIS LAND CALLED AMERICA: **VIRGINIA**

CREATIVE EDUCATION

Published by Creative Education

P.O. Box 227, Mankato, Minnesota 56002

Creative Education is an imprint of The Creative Company

www.thecreativecompany.us

Design by Blue Design (www.bluedes.com)

Art direction by Rita Marshall

Book production by The Design Lab

Printed in the United States of America

Photographs by Alamy (Classic Image, Mary Evans Picture Library, Witold Skyrypczak), Corbis (William A. Bake, Bettmann, Richard A. Cooke, Jay Dickman, The Gallery Collection, Karen Kasmauski, Medford Historical Society Collection, David Muench, Lynda Richardson, Rykoff Collection, Stapleton Collection, Underwood & Underwood, Dennis Whitehead, Tim Wright), Dreamstime (Marhow), Getty Images (James P. Blair, FPG, Joe Raedle, Medford Taylor), iStockphoto (Klaas Lingbeek-van Kranen)

Library of Congress Cataloging-in-Publication Data

Tougas, Joe.

Virginia / by Joe Tougas.

p. cm. — (This land called America)

Includes bibliographical references and index.

ISBN 978-1-58341-799-7

1. Virginia—Juvenile literature. I. Title. II. Series.

F226.3.T68 2009

975.5—dc22   2008009530

First Edition

9 8 7 6 5 4 3 2 1

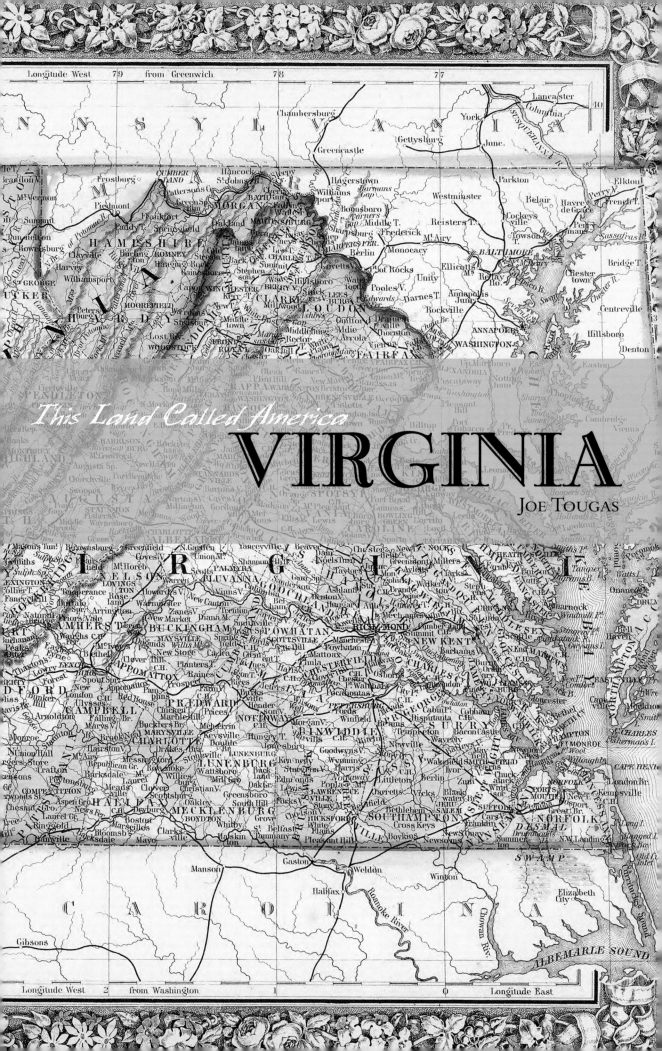

This Land Called America

VIRGINIA

Joe Tougas

THIS LAND CALLED AMERICA

Virginia

JOE TOUGAS

THE SEASON'S FIRST SNOWFALL HITS THE
BIRCH, MAPLE, AND WHITE PINE TREES OF THE
SHENANDOAH VALLEY IN NORTH-CENTRAL
VIRGINIA. TWO HIKERS TREK ALONG A FOREST
TRAIL, MARVELING THAT THIS BEAUTIFUL
WILDERNESS IS ONLY 100 MILES (160 KM) FROM
THE BUSTLE OF WASHINGTON, D.C. TO THEIR
RIGHT, THEY SEE A WHITE-TAILED DEER SCURRYING
AWAY. THE SOUND OF ITS RUNNING IS AS CLEAR AS
THE RIPPLE OF THE SHENANDOAH RIVER NEARBY.
THE HIKERS CONTINUE UP THE TRAIL, THEIR EYES
AND EARS ON THE ALERT FOR BOBCATS, BLACK
BEARS, AND OTHER ANIMALS THAT SHARE THE
RICH, COLORFUL VIRGINIA FOREST.

YEAR

1584 Explorer Walter Raleigh gives the name "Virginia" to land on the East Coast of North America.

EVENT

A Search for Riches

Long before Virginia became a state, explorers admired its majestic hills and powerful rivers. In the 1580s, English explorer Walter Raleigh named the region Virginia, after the nickname of England's Queen Elizabeth I. In the early 1600s, King James of England decided to establish

About 70 years after the English settled at Jamestown (opposite), they ran into intense conflict with local Indians (above).

Virginia as a colony. He believed the land was rich in gold, silver, and other goods that could be shipped back to England.

In 1606, the king sent three ships carrying 104 Englishmen to Virginia. They arrived five months later in 1607 and landed in a harbor now called Hampton Roads. They established the first permanent English colony in America at Jamestown.

The Europeans were not the first to live in this area, though. When the English settlers began turning Virginia into a colony, about 20,000 American Indians lived there. Most lived in small villages near rivers. They grew crops such as corn, beans, melons, and tobacco. The Powhatan tribe lived along the coast and did not believe in owning land, but the settlers who had arrived did. This became the cause of many conflicts.

YEAR
1607   The first permanent English colony in what will become the U.S. is established in Virginia.
EVENT

- 7 -

State bird: cardinal

The first settlers had arrived in Virginia at a bad time. It was too late in the year to plant crops. And because most of the English gentlemen who came to America were not good hunters or fishermen, food ran short during the winter. Many settlers died of starvation and from diseases such as malaria and pneumonia.

When the first supply ship arrived from Europe in 1608, only 38 of Jamestown's original settlers were still alive. But soon, English women sailed on ships to Virginia, and the men and women began forming families. Laws were passed that allowed settlers to own land if they grew crops on it. As a result, many people decided to become farmers. Work increased, and more food became available to buy and sell. The colony started to grow.

In the 1700s, many of Virginia's farms grew into plantations, which consisted of large homes and thousands of acres of land. Farmers on the plantations grew tobacco. They forced slaves captured from Africa to work in their fields.

As Virginia and the other 12 American colonies continued to grow, they began to desire independence from England. This led to the Revolutionary War, which began in 1775. The Americans were led in battle by Virginia native George Washington. After six years, America won the war. The colonies joined

In an act symbolizing surrender, English general Charles Cornwallis gave his sword to George Washington in 1781.

YEAR

1612 Farmer John Rolfe creates a new kind of tobacco that becomes very popular in Europe.

EVENT

Once they were freed, former slaves often didn't have places to live, so the government set up housing for them.

together to form the United States. On June 25, 1788, Virginia became the 10th American state. The following year, George Washington became the country's first president.

As the 19th century began, Virginia had the most slaves of any state in the nation. From 1861 to 1865, the issue of slavery divided the country as the North and South fought the Civil War. In 1861, Virginia joined other Southern, pro-slavery states in seceding from, or leaving, the Union. Virginia (which also included West Virginia at that time) was the site of the first and last major battles of the Civil War, which was won by the North in 1865.

Virginia was not allowed back into the Union until 1870. As the year 1900 approached, though, Virginia and other defeated Southern states slowly recovered from the destruction of war. They tried to adjust to a new era in which slavery was no longer legal.

Due to their location on key rivers, Virginia cities such as Yorktown were taken over by the Northern army.

YEAR

1619 The African slave trade begins in Virginia.

EVENT

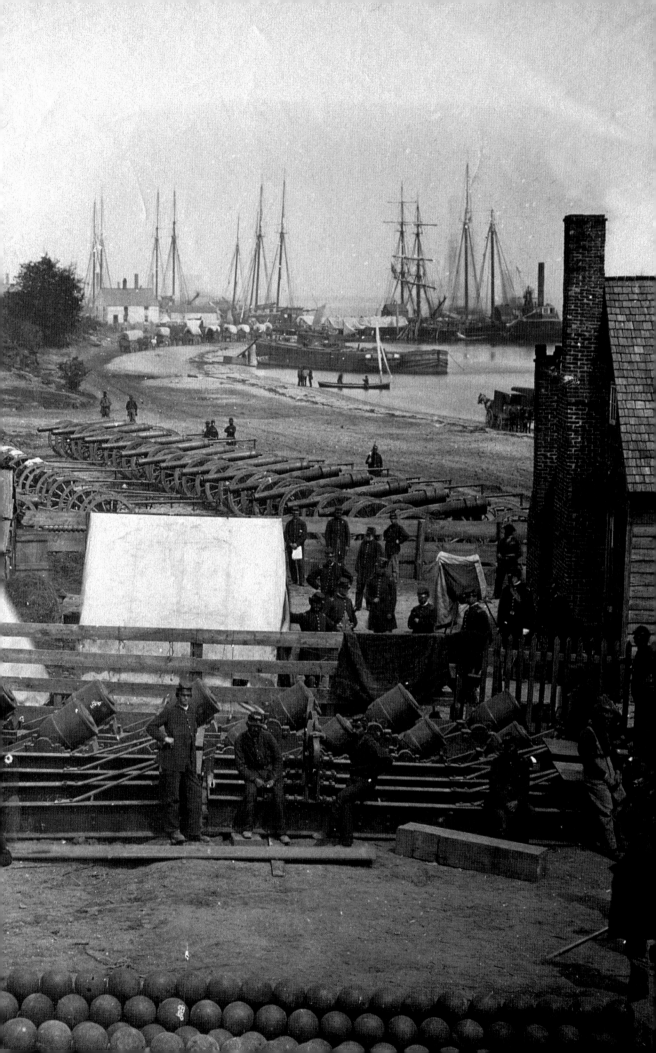

A Beautiful Scene

Virginia is located on the southeastern coast of the U.S. It is shaped like a triangle, with one side up against the Atlantic Ocean and two longer sides touched by several states. In the north, Virginia is bordered by Washington, D.C., and Maryland. West Virginia runs along its northwestern border, and

the western edge of the state touches Kentucky and Tennes-
see. The state of North Carolina lies to Virginia's south.

Virginia's varied landscape includes mountains, valleys, and
coastlines. With its entire eastern side bordering Chesapeake
Bay and the Atlantic Ocean, Virginia's Coastal Plain region is
made up of estuaries (bodies of water where the ocean mixes
with rivers) and peninsulas (pieces of land that jut out and
are almost entirely surrounded by water). Chesapeake Bay is
the biggest estuary in the U.S. It is a great spot to find clams,
blue crabs, and oysters.

Many powerful rivers also crisscross Virginia. These
include the James, Elizabeth, and Nansemond rivers. Toward
the eastern edge of the state, the rivers cross a long line of tall,
hard rocks called the Fall Line. As they flow over the Fall Line,
the rivers form cascading waterfalls and churning rapids.

*In addition to the many
waterfalls (above)
found along the Fall
Line, Virginia also
features small barrier
islands with short
coastlines (opposite).*

YEAR

1781   The Revolutionary War ends with English general Lord Charles Cornwallis's surrender at Yorktown.

EVENT

- 13 -

The Fall Line marks the border between the Coastal Plain and Piedmont regions. Important cities such as the capital of Richmond were founded just west of the Fall Line on the high ground of the Piedmont. This region is good for growing crops such as tobacco, corn, cotton, hay, and peanuts. West of the Piedmont are the Blue Ridge Mountains. The Blue Ridge is a range of the Appalachian Mountains that runs in a narrow band from north-central to southwestern Virginia. Mount Rogers, which is part of the Blue Ridge range, stands at an elevation of 5,729 feet (1,746 m) and is the highest point in the state.

West of the Blue Ridge Mountains is the Valley and Ridge region, which includes more mountains and the sweeping Valley of Virginia. The largest valley within the Valley of Virginia is the Shenandoah. Black bears, white-tailed deer, and bobcats roam the valley, which is covered with vibrant wildflowers such as azaleas and black-eyed Susans. The valley is also home to many poultry and dairy farms, as well as apple orchards.

Among other woodland creatures, white-tailed deer (above) can be found in the forested areas along the Shenandoah River (opposite) and throughout the valley of the same name.

YEAR

1788   Virginia becomes the 10th state on June 25.

EVENT

Coal miners sometimes use heavy-duty powered shovels to break the rock loose from underground mines.

Virginia's land contains a wealth of natural resources such as coal. Miners extract coal from underground mines, and the coal is burned for energy. Stone, sand, gravel, lime, and natural gas are other important resources in the state. Virginia is also the nation's only producer of "Virginia aplite," an important mineral used in making glass.

Although central Virginia has a more humid climate, the weather throughout the state is relatively mild. Virginia does not experience extreme high temperatures in the summer. It also does not get as cold as most northern states in the winter. The average temperature in the summer is between 70 and 80 °F (21 to 27 °C), and in the winter, it is 36 °F (2 °C).

However, Virginia does get occasional winter storms called "nor'easters." When violent winds blow in from the northeast, they bring lots of snow. At times, nor'easters have become so strong that they have been labeled "White Hurricanes." In January 1772, George Washington and Thomas Jefferson both recorded in their diaries that a nor'easter dropped about 33 inches (84 cm) of snow on central Virginia.

Richmond may be humid in the summer, but those who live on famed Monument Avenue live comfortably year-round.

YEAR

1789 Virginia native George Washington is elected as the first president of the U.S.

EVENT

- 17 -

People and Products

IN COLONIAL DAYS, MANY EUROPEANS CAME TO VIRGINIA IN SEARCH OF GOLD. OTHERS WERE YOUNGER SONS WHO CAME BECAUSE ENGLISH LAW ALLOWED ONLY THE OLDEST SON IN A FAMILY TO INHERIT HIS PARENTS' LAND. IN VIRGINIA, THESE MEN COULD HAVE THEIR OWN LAND. SOME SETTLERS CAME TO BRING THE CHRISTIAN RELIGION TO THE AMERICAN INDIANS.

Many of Virginia's original settlers were men who were not good at the type of hard work needed to thrive in a new territory. John Rolfe, however, knew how to survive and succeed. He was the first to grow and sell tobacco, a crop that made the colony rich in the 1600s. Rolfe also married Pocahontas, the daughter of a Powhatan chief.

Today, growing tobacco remains a top industry in Virginia. The state ranks fifth among tobacco-growing states. The largest tobacco company in the U.S., Philip Morris USA, employs almost 6,000 Virginians and is among the state's 50 largest employers.

Tobacco, which is often used to make cigarettes (above), was a booming business in early 1900s Richmond (opposite).

YEAR

1861   Virginia secedes from the Union at the start of the Civil War.

EVENT

Apart from Philip Morris, which belongs to the larger Altria Group, a number of other major corporations are also located in the state. Many companies have their corporate headquarters in Richmond, including Hamilton Beach, a manufacturer of small kitchen appliances. America's top newspaper publisher, Gannett, is headquartered in McLean. Nearby, in Reston, is the state's biggest moneymaker, Sprint Nextel.

With the state's good business climate, it is no wonder that many Virginians work in the computer software industry and other high-tech jobs in bioscience and communications. About 3,000 technology-related companies are located in Virginia. The largest concentration of computer companies is in northern Virginia. More than 1,100 firms, including Internet service providers such as AOL, can be found there.

Gannett publishes 85 daily newspapers, such as USA Today, and almost 900 non-daily papers throughout the U.S.

YEAR
1865
EVENT

Confederate general Robert E. Lee surrenders at Appomattox Court House, ending the Civil War.

The Virginia-born presidents, beginning with the top row, from left to right: Washington, Madison, Jefferson, Monroe, Harrison, Tyler, Taylor, and Wilson.

Low-tech products are also manufactured in Virginia. Clothing and food products are produced in the state's capital of Richmond. Furniture and fabric are made in southern Virginia. Along the Atlantic coast, Newport News, Hampton, and Norfolk are shipbuilding centers.

With so many different industries, Virginia is home to a wide variety of people. About 73 percent of the state's population of 7.7 million is white. African Americans make up about 20 percent of the population. Asian Americans are the third-largest group, at nearly five percent of the population.

Among the people to have called Virginia home have been a number of important leaders. Virginia is sometimes called "The Mother of Presidents" because more U.S. presidents were born there than in any other state. George Washington, James Madison, Thomas Jefferson, James Monroe, William Henry Harrison, John Tyler, Zachary Taylor, and Woodrow Wilson were all born in Virginia.

Another important Virginian was Booker T. Washington, who is best remembered for helping many African Americans

At Northrop Grumman Shipbuilding, a shipyard in Newport News, large cargo ships are built and repaired.

YEAR
1870   Virginia rejoins the Union after being banned from statehood for five years after the Civil War.
EVENT

succeed after slavery. Washington was born into slavery in 1856 and was nine years old when slavery was outlawed. He grew up to become an instructor at Hampton Institute, a school for black children. Later, he headed the Tuskegee Institute in Alabama (now called Tuskegee University), a historically African American college.

Another notable African American from Virginia was tennis great Arthur Ashe. He was the first black person to ever win the U.S. Open and the Wimbledon Men's Singles. By the 1970s, he was among the most famous tennis players in the world. But tennis wasn't his only pursuit. Ashe fought passionately against South Africa's system of apartheid, which were laws that kept non-white South Africans separate from whites by barring them from certain jobs and obstructing opportunities for education and health care.

A fierce competitor on the tennis court, Arthur Ashe could not defeat AIDS, from which he died in 1993.

YEAR

1913   Virginia native Woodrow Wilson becomes the 28th president of the U.S.

EVENT

A Proud State

Virginia is a state rich in historical sites. Mount Vernon, the home of president George Washington before and after the Revolutionary War, is located on the Potomac River in eastern Virginia. Every year, millions of visitors tour the 500-acre (202 ha) "Mansion House Farm." Washington and his wife, Martha, are both buried on the grounds.

Those more interested in the Civil War can visit the village of Appomattox Court House. It was there that the South surrendered to the North to end the Civil War. The home of Wilmer and Virginia McLean, where generals Ulysses S. Grant and Robert E. Lee agreed to the surrender, is open to the public for tours.

After the Civil War, Arlington National Cemetery was created as a burial ground for those who had died in the war. It is now the largest national cemetery and includes the graves of thousands of military men and women who served the U.S. in wartime. The cemetery also holds the Tomb of the Unknowns, which is dedicated to unidentified U.S. soldiers who died in each conflict from World War I through Vietnam (1914–1975).

Near Arlington National Cemetery stands the Pentagon, home to the U.S. Department of Defense. This five-sided building was a target of the terrorist attacks of September 11, 2001. On that day, terrorists hijacked a Boeing 757 jet airliner and crashed it into the Pentagon. The attack killed 184 people, including 59 who were on the plane.

Two well-known landmarks in Virginia are George Washington's estate at Mount Vernon (opposite) and the Pentagon (above).

YEAR

1941   The Pentagon is built near Arlington as the headquarters of the U.S. Department of Defense.

EVENT

Chesapeake Bay fisherman

I n addition to its importance as a site for government operations, Virginia is also a popular destination for special events. The Shenandoah Apple Blossom Festival takes place in Winchester every May. This community celebration of music, dance, and art welcomes the arrival of spring. The three-day Hampton Jazz Festival, which has featured some of the nation's top jazz musicians since 1968, is held every June. And in August, fiddlers from around the world gather for the Old Fiddlers' Convention in Galax.

Virginia's beautiful landscape also draws sightseers and adventurers carrying backpacks and cameras. The mountains and valleys are ideal for hiking and camping, while the seashore attracts fishermen, sailors, and swimmers. One of the state's most popular attractions is Mount Rogers, which is an ideal spot for hiking, mountain biking, and horseback riding.

On Virginia's eastern shore, Chesapeake Bay fishermen harvest blue crabs (above), and west of the Blue Ridge Mountains, festivals are held in communities in the Shenandoah Valley (opposite).

Virginia's schools are desegregated, allowing black and white children to attend school together.

QUICK FACTS

Population: 7,712,091

Largest city: Virginia Beach (pop. 434,743)

Capital: Richmond

Entered the union: June 25, 1788

Nicknames: Old Dominion, Mother of Presidents

State flower: flowering dogwood

State bird: cardinal

Size: 42,774 sq mi (110,706 sq km)—35th-biggest in U.S.

Major industries: agriculture, manufacturing, technology

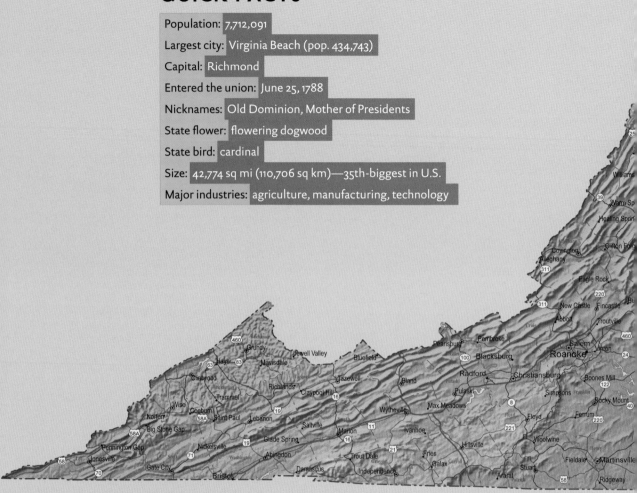

In addition to participating in outdoor adventures, Virginians enjoy watching their favorite sports teams in action. Although there are no professional teams in the state, Virginia's sports fans root for the state's 11 Division I college teams. Among them are the Hokies of Virginia Tech, whose football squads made several appearances in college bowl games in the 1990s.

Auto racing is also popular with Virginians. There are several NASCAR (National Association for Stock Car Auto Racing) tracks in Richmond and Martinsville. The Richmond

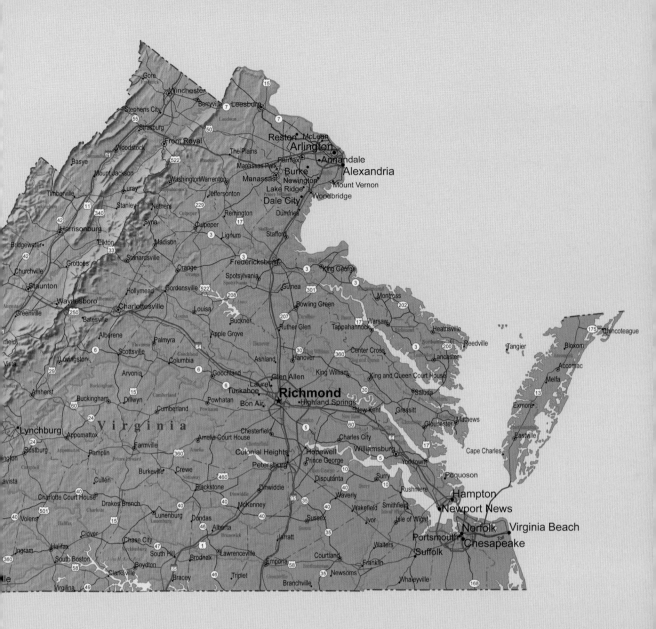

International Raceway has been hosting races and other events since NASCAR was formed in 1948.

From auto racing to software design, Virginia is a state offering both fast action and quiet, technical advancements. As a state that held key roles in America's past, Virginia will always be of strong interest to visitors from around the world who want to see and learn more about the U.S. With a rich history shaped by hardships, sacrifice, and triumph, Virginia is moving confidently toward a promising future.

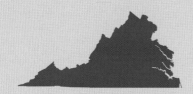

BIBLIOGRAPHY

Blashfield, Jean. *Virginia*. New York: Grolier Publishing, 1998.

Davis, William C., and James I. Robertson Jr. *Virginia at War, 1862*. Lexington, Kent.: University Press of Kentucky, 2007.

Lange, Karen E. *1607: A New Look at Jamestown*. Washington, D.C.: National Geographic, 2007.

National Park Service. "Shenandoah National Park." National Park Service, U.S. Department of the Interior. http://www.nps.gov/shen.

Rubin, Louis D. *Virginia: A History*. New York: W. W. Norton and Company, 1984.

INDEX